European Travel Journal

*If you are lucky enough to have lived in
Paris as a young man, then wherever you go
for the rest of your life it stays with you,
for Paris is a moveable feast.*

—ERNEST HEMINGWAY

EUROPEAN TRAVEL JOURNAL

TEN SPEED PRESS
Berkeley Toronto

Ten Speed Press
P.O. Box 7123
Berkeley, California 94707
www.tenspeed.com

A Kirsty Melville book

Distributed in Australia by Simon & Schuster Australia,
in Canada by Ten Speed Press Canada, in New Zealand by
Southern Publishers Group, in South Africa by Real Books, in
Southeast Asia by Berkeley Books, and in the United Kingdom
and Europe by Airlift Book Company.

Cover illustration and design by Kathy Warinner
Interior design by Libby Oda

Telephone numbers, addresses, and Web site URLs are
correct at the time of going to press and may be subject
to subsequent alteration.

ISBN 1-58008-184-3

First printing, 2000
Printed in Canada

1 2 3 4 5 6 7 8 9 10 — 04 03 02 01 00

CONTENTS

Personal
Information

Personal Data ....

Name ....

Address and phone ....

....

Overseas address and phone ....

....

In case of emergency, please contact ....

....

....

Blood group ....

Special medical information ....

....

....

....

....

Religion ....

Passport number ....

Air ticket numbers ....

....

....

....

....

....

....

....

PACKING CHECKLIST

- ○ adapter(s)/converter(s)
- ○ alarm clock/watch
- ○ bandanna
- ○ binoculars
- ○ camera/batteries/film
- ○ clothesline
- ○ credit cards
- ○ drain stopper
- ○ driver's license
- ○ earplugs
- ○ eyeshade
- ○ flashlight
- ○ glasses/contacts (spare)
- ○ guidebooks
- ○ hanger (inflatable)
- ○ itineraries
- ○ lock
- ○ maps
- ○ money belt
- ○ passport (and photocopy)
- ○ pen
- ○ plastic bags
- ○ prescriptions
- ○ (eyeglass/medicines)
- ○ safety pins
- ○ sewing kit
- ○ sleep sack
- ○ string bag (for shopping/laundry)
- ○ student I.D. card
- ○ sunglasses
- ○ swimsuit
- ○ Swiss army knife
- ○ travel journal

Other things you may consider taking with you are: a small photo album or "talking book," to show people you meet where you come from and what your family and friends look like; inexpensive little gifts, e.g., stamps, chewing gum, picture postcards from home, to give new acquaintances; and some of your business or calling cards.

PACKING TIPS

* Keep your color scheme simple.

* Set out everything you think you must bring—and eliminate half.

* Two or three bottoms and three or four tops should see you through almost every situation.

* Fold up silk shirts in plastic bags to avoid wrinkles.

* Keep accessories to a bare minimum and do not bring good jewelry or other valuables.

Adapted from Judith Gilford, *The Packing Book*

HEALTH TIPS

* No special vaccinations are usually needed for travel in Europe. If you will be traveling elsewhere, check with the Center for Disease Control in Atlanta, which keeps the most up-to-date records of health conditions and required inoculations abroad. Call (404) 332-4559 or (404) 332-4555. Or order their annual report, "Health Information for International Travel," from the Government Printing Office, Washington, DC 20402. Then consult with your doctor regarding inoculations and other health precautions you should take before leaving.

* Also, The International Association for Medical Assistance to Travelers (IAMAT) has a chart of recommended immunizations for more than 200 countries, and an international directory of English-speaking doctors.
In the US: 417 Center St., Lewiston, NY 14092; (716) 754-4883. In Canada: 40 Regal Rd., Guelph, Ont N1K 1B5; (519) 836-0102

* Check your health insurance coverage: purchase additional travel coverage if necessary.

* Drink water only from factory-sealed bottles.
* If the water is questionable, then so is ice, fruits, vegetables, dishes, or cutlery.
* To purify water boil it, use a portable microfilter, such as PUR, or use iodine tablets (follow package directions and don't use if you are allergic or pregnant).
* Keep prescription medications in their original bottles.
* Pack copies of all prescriptions.
* Bring your doctor's phone, fax, and/or e-mail address.

First Aid and
Toiletries Checklist

❍ adhesive bandages
❍ antacid
❍ antihistamine
❍ aspirin/Tylenol
❍ calamine lotion
❍ comb/brush
❍ condoms/dental dams
❍ contact lens solution
❍ contraceptives
❍ dental floss
❍ deodorant
❍ diarrhea/indigestion remedies
❍ hair dryer
❍ insect repellant
❍ laundry soap
❍ laxative
❍ lip balm
❍ menstrual cramp remedy

❍ moleskin
❍ motion sickness remedy
❍ nail clippers
❍ nail file
❍ prescription medicines
❍ razor
❍ shampoo
❍ shower sandals
❍ skin lotion
❍ soap
❍ sunscreen
❍ tampons/pads
❍ toilet paper
❍ toothbrush
❍ toothpaste
❍ towel/washcloth
❍ water purification tablets or filters

NATURAL REMEDIES
FOR TRAVELERS

Bladder infection	cranberry juice
Bruises or strained muscles	arnica salve
Diarrhea	mint tea; "pill curing" (Chinese herb combination); Wakefield Blackberry Root Tincture
Hangover	nux vomica; "pill curing" (Chinese herb combination)
Headache	nux vomica
Jet lag	"pill curing" (Chinese herb combination)
Menstrual cramps	lobelia tincture; dong quai
Mosquito repellent	(topical)chrysanthemum extract; citronella; lemon eucalyptus oil; pennyroyal
Mosquito repellent (take internally)	Vitamin B
Motion sickness	powdered ginger capsules
Poison ivy or oak	echinacea (taken internally)
Skin injury (burns, bug bites, rashes, cuts)	California Gel; echinacea salve
Stomach upset	chamomile
Stress	avena; chamomile; chrysanthemum; ginseng; passion-flower
Sunburn	aloe vera; ching wan hung (Chinese herb); vitamin B
Yeast infections	acidophilus; citrus fruit; plain yogurt (taken internally)

Adapted from Thalia Zepatos, *A Journey of One's Own*
and Dr. Barry Rose, *The Family Health Guide to Homeopathy*

TRAVEL GUIDES AND
WEB SITES

The seeds of civilization are in every culture,
but it is city life that brings them to fruition.

—SUSANNE K. LANGER

For up-to-date information check out the following Web sites for general information about European travel: accommodations; youth hostels; hotels; beds and breakfasts; resorts; rail and auto transportation in Europe; air travel to and from Europe; health and issues in Europe.

The Virtual Tourist

www.vtourist.com

A "Travel Directory" that combines broad practical information and travel tools with a sense of community and the art of travel.

Rough Guide to Travel

www.roughguides.com

In addition to offering information on over 4,000 locations, this is the home of one of the best travel message boards on the Web: "The Rough Guide Journal."

Travelocity

www.travelocity.com

Parented by Sabre, the computerized reservation system, Travelocity offers a full range of reservation services and all the travel support an agency provides. Note the "Fare Watcher" e-mail service.

CNN Travel Guide

www.cnn.com/TRAVEL

This is a full-service travel Web site and includes "City Guides." Select a major national or international city from the "City Guides" menu for a comprehensive and current rundown on what you'll find there.

RecTravel Library

www.travelmate.com

Essential travel information links combined with an excellent collection of travelogues.

Eurotrip.com

www.eurotrip.com

This site focuses on backpacking through Europe with an emphasis on hostelry, rail travel, and bargains.

Frommer's Budget Travel Online

www.frommers.com

Splashy, commercial site with a lot to offer, including international destination guides, low-cost fares, and trip preparation.

Travlang

www.travlang.com

Known for their foreign language tutorials (over 70 languages) and translating dictionaries, Travlang also has a useful menu of travel-related services.

TravelWeb

www.travelweb.com

Commercial site with good information about transportation and lodging worldwide.

Virtual Library: West European Studies Home Page

www.pitt.edu/~wwwes/

Although an academically oriented site heavily weighted with European Union information, this site also contains current news summaries for individual countries and travel news.

Excellent guidebooks for the countries of Europe are:

Fodor's Guides
Berkeley Guides
Lonely Planet
Let's Go

ITINERARY

If we are always arriving and departing, it is also true that we are eternally anchored. One's destination is never a place but rather a new way of looking at things.

—HENRY MILLER

DATE ....

   Depart ....

   Arrive ....

   Accommodations ....

DATE ....

   Depart ....

   Arrive ....

   Accommodations ....

DATE ....

   Depart ....

   Arrive ....

   Accommodations ....

DATE ....

   Depart ....

   Arrive ....

   Accommodations ....

DATE ....

   Depart ....

   Arrive ....

   Accommodations ....

DATE ....

   Depart ....

   Arrive ....

   Accommodations ....

ITINERARY

DATE ....

    Depart ....

    Arrive ....

    Accommodations ....

DATE ....

    Depart ....

    Arrive ....

    Accommodations ....

DATE ....

    Depart ....

    Arrive ....

    Accommodations ....

DATE ....

    Depart ....

    Arrive ....

    Accommodations ....

DATE ....

    Depart ....

    Arrive ....

    Accommodations ....

DATE ....

    Depart ....

    Arrive ....

    Accommodations ....

DATE ....

    Depart ....

    Arrive ....

    Accommodations ....

ITINERARY

DATE ....

    Depart ....

    Arrive ....

    Accommodations ....

DATE ....

    Depart ....

    Arrive ....

    Accommodations ....

DATE ....

    Depart ....

    Arrive ....

    Accommodations ....

DATE ....

    Depart ....

    Arrive ....

    Accommodations ....

DATE ....

    Depart ....

    Arrive ....

    Accommodations ....

DATE ....

    Depart ....

    Arrive ....

    Accommodations ....

DATE ....

    Depart ....

    Arrive ....

    Accommodations ....

Money and Currency Exchange

... to the city where the air trembled like
a tuning-fork with unimaginable possibilities.

—Willa Cather

It's best to carry a combination of traveler's checks, credit cards, and cash

Traveler's checks are safe and often receive a better exchange rate than cash. However, it's difficult to be reimbursed for lost traveler's checks without an accurate record of traveler's checks bought and cashed. Your record should include location and date of purchases and should be updated every evening.

ATM (Automatic Teller Machine) systems give you access to cash from your checking account, or you can charge to your credit card. These machines also offer good exchange rates.

Check with your bank to make sure that your ATM access code will work. Note that most ATMs in Europe accept four-digit codes.

Know the local currency. Study the coins and bills so that you are comfortable making transactions. Change does not usually convert back to U.S. currency. When first arriving, buy something that you know the price of well back home—for example, a soda or a magazine. This will give you practice getting change in the new currency and knowing how it converts.

Obtain some cash in the currency of the country you are traveling to before your departure. This is not the way to get a good exchange rate, of course, but you'll be glad you thought ahead if there are any difficulties upon arrival.

Also carry about $50 in U.S. currency which will be useful on your return.

LEARN HOW THE EXCHANGE SYSTEM WORKS

Look for the best exchange rate, usually found at local banks, American Express or Thomas Cook offices, and ATMs. Generally avoid changing money in hotels or shops.

In general, travelers get the best exchange rates when using credit cards or debit cards. To find out more, and to find out about special cards for travelers, contact the following:

Visa: www.visa.com or 1-800-227-6811

Mastercard: www.mastercard.com or 1-800-307-7309

American Express: www.americanexpress.com or
1-800-258-4800

Don't be overly concerned with the different rates offered and fluctuations in the exchange rate-often it doesn't amount to much money. Carry a calculator and just keep an eye on what you're paying for money.

Save receipts of money exchanged. Many countries require these receipts if you want to change local currency back to U.S. dollars at the end of your trip.

RECOMMENDED WEB SITES FOR CURRENCY EXCHANGE RATE

(www.travlang.com/money) This site has the latest currency exchange rates, a JavaScript calculator, recent historical perspectives, and interesting information about each currency.

BE AWARE OF DUTY CHARGES

Obtain from "Know Before You Go" a list of duty charges, from the U.S. Customs Service, 1301 Constitution Avenue NW, Washington, DC 20229-0001. (www.customs. ustreas.gov)

"GSP and the International Traveler" (www.customs. gov/travel/travel.htm) explains duty exemption under the Generalized System of Preferences.

A NOTE ABOUT THE EURO

The fifteen European countries on the next page have set aside tradition and nationalism for the practical benefits of a single currency. The "Euro" was officially born January 1,

1999. This is when the clock started on a three-year changeover, to culminate with the circulation of the new notes and coins in 2002.

How will this historic change affect the traveler? Favorably, for the most part, for two reasons. First, ease of travel. A U.S. citizen on a tour of Europe will only have to change money once—at least if he enters within the fifteen European Union member countries. Second, the cost of changing money each time he enters a new country will be eliminated.

THE EURO

Austria
Belgium
Denmark
Finland
France
Germany
Greece
Ireland
Italy
Luxembourg
The Netherlands
Portugal
Spain
Sweden
United Kingdom

Less certain is how the Euro will hold up to the dollar. If it is relatively strong, some travel bargains may lose their luster.

Record of Traveler's Checks
and Credit Cards

*"The honor of that moment," the King went on,
"I shall never, never forget!" "You will though," the Queen
said, "if you don't make a memorandum of it."*

—Lewis Carroll, *Through the Looking Glass*

Lost or Stolen Traveler's Checks

Dial Collect from Anywhere in the World
American Express (800) 528-4800
Citicorp (800) 645-6556 or (813) 623-1709
Mastercard International/Thomas Cook (609) 987-730
Visa (410) 481-7911

From within the U.S.
American Express (800) 221-7282
Citicorp (800) 645-6556
Mastercard International/Thomas Cook (800) 223-7373
Visa (800) VISA-911

Number	Amount	Date & Place Cashed	Exchange Rate

RECORD OF TRAVELER'S CHECKS AND CREDIT CARDS

Number	Amount	Date & Place Cashed	Exchange Rate

CREDIT CARD NUMBERS ....

....

....

Addresses

Name ....
  Address ....
  Telephone ....
  E-mail ....

Name ....
  Address ....
  Telephone ....
  E-mail ....

Name ....
  Address ....
  Telephone ....
  E-mail ....

Name ....
  Address ....
  Telephone ....
  E-mail ....

Name ....
  Address ....
  Telephone ....
  E-mail ....

Name ....
  Address ....
  Telephone ....
  E-mail ....

Name ....
  Address ....
  Telephone ....
  E-mail ....

Addresses

NAME ....
   Address ....
   Telephone ....
   E-mail ....

NAME ....
   Address ....
   Telephone ....
   E-mail ....

NAME ....
   Address ....
   Telephone ....
   E-mail ....

NAME ....
   Address ....
   Telephone ....
   E-mail ....

NAME ....
   Address ....
   Telephone ....
   E-mail ....

NAME ....
   Address ....
   Telephone ....
   E-mail ....

NAME ....
   Address ....
   Telephone ....
   E-mail ....

Addresses

Name ....
   Address ....
   Telephone ....
   E-mail ....

Name ....
   Address ....
   Telephone ....
   E-mail ....

Name ....
   Address ....
   Telephone ....
   E-mail ....

Name ....
   Address ....
   Telephone ....
   E-mail ....

Name ....
   Address ....
   Telephone ....
   E-mail ....

Name ....
   Address ....
   Telephone ....
   E-mail ....

Name ....
   Address ....
   Telephone ....
   E-mail ....

ᴀADDRESSES

Nᴀᴍᴇ ....
   Address ....
   Telephone ....
   E-mail ....

Nᴀᴍᴇ ....
   Address ....
   Telephone ....
   E-mail ....

Nᴀᴍᴇ ....
   Address ....
   Telephone ....
   E-mail ....

Nᴀᴍᴇ ....
   Address ....
   Telephone ....
   E-mail ....

Nᴀᴍᴇ ....
   Address ....
   Telephone ....
   E-mail ....

Nᴀᴍᴇ ....
   Address ....
   Telephone ....
   E-mail ....

Nᴀᴍᴇ ....
   Address ....
   Telephone ....
   E-mail ....

Writing While
Exploring

Writing is a way of talking without being interrupted.

—Jules Renard

There is a wonderful symbiosis between traveling and writing. Finding a good time to write as you travel is as important as selecting the subject that you want to write about in your journal. Subjects can be a simple recounting of the day's activities or, for the more courageous writer, illustrious observations of all that is spontaneous and new in each day of travel. We asked author and teacher John Timpane to help us out. Below find his thoughts and tips on keeping a journal to get you started.

Keeping a Journal

People have all sorts of reasons for writing a journal while traveling. For most, it is capturing the newness of an experience when it occurs. Whether it be the first sight of some spectacular building or horizon, local foods that are different and hard to describe, the occasional disaster, or the friends made on the road, recording it adds to our memories all that is striking on our trip.

There's no one way to write a journal. There are those who try to write everything down. Everything. A friend said, "I spend the first half of the day traveling, and the second half writing about what happened in the first half." Some takes notes to help in recounting later when there is more time to expand on a thought. Some write down every photograph and expense. The possibilities go on.

The art of journal writing involves finding a balance between the discipline of writing and the spontaneity of traveling. Writing regularly, every day, is important—probably essential. But traveling does not usually lend itself to a strict writing regimen. Remember that your journal is there when you find yourself with those unplanned blocks of time, for instance, when waiting for the next train because you missed the one you wanted, (or for a flight that is delayed). You finish touring early and you are waiting for the group, or maybe you are too early to be let in to your hotel room.

WAYS TO GET STARTED

* *Write as if you were speaking to another.* Someone back home or a family member you are directing your thoughts to. No reason to stretch for poetry or profundity. They'll come if they're there. The plain facts, stated in your own voice, can be very effective.

* *Make up a friend or an imaginary addressee.* Write the journal as though it is to this person. Entries can become very personal and intimate in this format.

* *Freewriting.* Decide not to have a plan for what to write about. Take a word and start from there. Write for $7^1/_2$ minutes. Don't ask why, just do it. Pay attention to any urges. Follow them. Veer off into observation or a story for the day.

* *Annotated itinerary.* It's a trifle cut-and-dried, but it can be fun. Go hour by hour and for each hour list at least two things you did and comment on at least one. (Some activities, such as a walking tour of Lisbon or an opera in Paris, will span hours, but the rules are the same.) List two things that happened to you that hour. And then a comment. Pay attention to what you did and what you thought about and be sure to write it down.

* *Five first things.* Write the five things that first pop into your head. Don't ask why, just do it, but leave a few lines between each of the five entries. Now, go back and expand on them. Why those particular five things? The excitement is in the discovery, and the discovery is most of the joy.

* *Sensory tour.* Start by using two of your five senses. Visual is a given. Taste is a good follow-up. (You'll be eating at some point.) Smell is always the trickiest, but with a little concentrated attention smell will start to clarify itself and become more possible to describe. Sounds are also

fascinating—take notice. Overheard conversations can count for sounds. Record. Tell stories if the senses have stories to tell.

* *Take a Polaroid camera.* Have an instant snapshot to paste in your journal and have the entry be a description of the picture. If not a picture, paste in train stubs, hotel receipts, or used theater tickets, and start the descriptions from these. Every stub and receipt stands for something you did.

* *Question & answer.* If you have a travel partner, ask questions interview style at the end of the day you shared. Make up a few questions in your journal, leave a few lines in between for the answers you get. Leave some extra room, as well, for your response to the answer. (Disagreements can lead to the best essays.)

* *The emotion journey.* Travel is famous for eliciting very pronounced emotions, often for reasons hard to know. Sometimes you will find yourself in a particular state due to very concrete things that happened to you in the day ("It was not pleasant when our haywagon collapsed into the lake.") At other times the connection might be deeper. ("After all those miles I realize how big the world is and how little I know about it.") Begin with just your emotional state and trace it somewhere. Each day start your writing entry by identifying your mood (happy, weary, excited, lonely, homesick, frustrated, afraid). Then try to trace the emotion to its source. Find something in the day or the place that has caused the feeling. ("Arrived in Paris and I just realized who I really love and she is 6,000 miles away. She should be here.") Pay attention to feelings and where they lead.

In fact, "pay attention" is the main rule of journal writing. Travel fills your days with new signs, new thoughts about the world, about yourself. New emotions. You'll never get all of them down. The idea is to record those that, later, when you reread your journal, will recreate the journey, and you will have all of it. Travel with eyes wide open. It's a great way to write, and not a bad way to live.

~ JOURNAL CONTENTS ~

Writing to me is a voyage, an odyssey, a discovery,
because I'm never certain of precisely what I will find.

—GABRIEL FIELDING

At the end of your travels (or as you go), use the lines below
to set up a table of contents for your journal.

SUBJECT/PLACE ....

BEGINS ON PAGE ....

SUBJECT/PLACE ....

BEGINS ON PAGE ....

SUBJECT/PLACE ....

BEGINS ON PAGE ....

SUBJECT/PLACE ....

BEGINS ON PAGE ....

SUBJECT/PLACE ....

BEGINS ON PAGE ....

SUBJECT/PLACE ....

BEGINS ON PAGE ....

SUBJECT/PLACE ....

BEGINS ON PAGE ....

SUBJECT/PLACE ....

BEGINS ON PAGE ....

DATE _____

PLACE _____

....

....

....

....

....

....

....

....

....

....

....

....

....

....

....

....

....

....

....

....

....

....

DATE _____

PLACE _____

. . . .

. . . .

. . . .

. . . .

. . . .

. . . .

. . . .

. . . .

. . . .

. . . .

. . . .

. . . .

. . . .

. . . .

. . . .

. . . .

. . . .

. . . .

. . . .

. . . .

. . . .

. . . .

DATE ______________________________

PLACE ______________________________

How can I know what I think till I see what I say?

—E. M. FORSTER

DATE _____

PLACE _____

. . . .

. . . .

. . . .

. . . .

. . . .

. . . .

. . . .

. . . .

. . . .

. . . .

. . . .

. . . .

. . . .

. . . .

. . . .

. . . .

. . . .

. . . .

. . . .

. . . .

. . . .

DATE _____

PLACE _____

. . . .

. . . .

. . . .

. . . .

. . . .

. . . .

. . . .

. . . .

. . . .

. . . .

. . . .

. . . .

. . . .

. . . .

. . . .

. . . .

. . . .

. . . .

. . . .

. . . .

DATE

PLACE

DATE _____

PLACE _____

. . . .

. . . .

. . . .

. . . .

. . . .

. . . .

. . . .

. . . .

. . . .

. . . .

. . . .

Writing is not apart from living.
Writing is a kind of double living.

—CATHERINE DRINKER BOWEN

. . . .

. . . .

. . . .

. . . .

. . . .

. . . .

. . . .

. . . .

DATE _____

PLACE _____

DATE _____

PLACE _____

. . . .

. . . .

. . . .

. . . .

. . . .

. . . .

. . . .

. . . .

. . . .

. . . .

. . . .

. . . .

. . . .

. . . .

. . . .

. . . .

. . . .

. . . .

. . . .

. . . .

. . . .

. . . .

DATE _____

PLACE _____

DATE _____

PLACE _____

. . . .

. . . .

. . . .

. . . .

. . . .

. . . .

. . . .

. . . .

. . . .

The writer must write what he has to say, not speak it.

—ERNEST HEMINGWAY

. . . .

. . . .

. . . .

. . . .

. . . .

. . . .

. . . .

. . . .

. . . .

. . . .

. . . .

DATE _____

PLACE _____

DATE _____

PLACE _____

....

....

....

....

....

....

....

....

....

....

....

....

....

....

....

....

....

....

....

....

....

....

DATE

PLACE

DATE _____

PLACE _____

. . . .

. . . .

. . . .

. . . .

. . . .

. . . .

. . . .

. . . .

. . . .

*The real voyage of discovery consists not in seeking
new landscapes, but in having new eyes.*

—MARCEL PROUST

. . . .

. . . .

. . . .

. . . .

. . . .

. . . .

. . . .

. . . .

. . . .

. . . .

DATE _____

PLACE _____

DATE _____

PLACE _____

....

....

....

....

....

....

....

....

....

....

....

....

....

....

....

....

....

....

....

....

....

DATE _____

PLACE _____

DATE _____

PLACE _____

....

....

....

....

....

....

....

....

....

We need only travel to give our intellects an airing.

—H. D. THOREAU

....

....

....

....

....

....

....

....

....

....

DATE _____

PLACE _____

. . . .

. . . .

. . . .

. . . .

. . . .

. . . .

. . . .

. . . .

. . . .

. . . .

. . . .

. . . .

. . . .

. . . .

. . . .

. . . .

. . . .

. . . .

. . . .

. . . .

. . . .

DATE _____

PLACE _____

DATE _____

PLACE _____

DATE _____

PLACE _____

....

....

....

....

....

....

....

....

....

Better to write for yourself and have no public,
than to write for the public and have no self.

—CYRIL CONNOLLY

....

....

....

....

....

....

....

....

....

....

DATE

PLACE

DATE _____

PLACE _____

....

....

....

....

....

....

....

....

....

....

....

....

....

....

....

....

....

....

....

....

....

....

DATE

PLACE

DATE _____

PLACE _____

....

....

....

....

....

....

....

....

....

The most beautiful things are those that
madness prompts and reason writes.

—ANDRÉ GIDE

....

....

....

....

....

....

....

....

....

....

DATE _____

PLACE _____

....

....

....

....

....

....

....

....

....

....

....

....

....

....

....

....

....

....

....

....

....

DATE _____

PLACE _____

DATE

PLACE

DATE _____

PLACE _____

....

....

....

....

....

....

....

....

....

There is no perfect time to write. There's only now.

—BARBARA KINGSOLVER

....

....

....

....

....

....

....

....

....

....

....

DATE _____

PLACE _____

DATE _____

PLACE _____

....

....

....

....

....

....

....

....

....

....

....

....

....

....

....

....

....

....

....

....

....

....

DATE _____

PLACE _____

DATE _____

PLACE _____

....

....

....

....

....

....

....

....

....

*Some writers confuse authenticity, which they
ought always to aim at, with originality,
which they should never bother about.*

—W. H. AUDEN

....

....

....

....

....

....

....

....

....

....

DATE _____

PLACE _____

DATE _____

PLACE _____

DATE

PLACE

DATE _____

PLACE _____

. . . .

. . . .

. . . .

. . . .

. . . .

. . . .

. . . .

. . . .

. . . .

*A man may write at any time if he will
set himself doggedly to it.*

—SAMUEL JOHNSON

. . . .

. . . .

. . . .

. . . .

. . . .

. . . .

. . . .

. . . .

. . . .

DATE

PLACE

DATE _____

PLACE _____

DATE _____

PLACE _____

DATE _____

PLACE _____

. . . .

. . . .

. . . .

. . . .

. . . .

. . . .

. . . .

. . . .

. . . .

One writes to make a home for oneself, on paper,
in time, in others' minds.

—ALFRED KAZIN

. . . .

. . . .

. . . .

. . . .

. . . .

. . . .

. . . .

. . . .

. . . .

. . . .

DATE _____

PLACE _____

....
....
....
....
....
....
....
....
....
....
....
....
....
....
....
....
....
....
....
....
....
....

DATE _____

PLACE _____

DATE _____

PLACE _____

. . . .

. . . .

. . . .

. . . .

. . . .

. . . .

. . . .

. . . .

. . . .

*I write for myself and strangers. The strangers,
dear Readers, are an afterthought.*

—GERTRUDE STEIN

. . . .

. . . .

. . . .

. . . .

. . . .

. . . .

. . . .

. . . .

. . . .

DATE

PLACE

DATE _____

PLACE_____

....

....

....

....

....

....

....

....

....

....

....

....

....

....

....

....

....

....

....

....

....

DATE _____

PLACE _____

....
....
....
....
....
....
....
....
....
....
....
....
....
....
....
....
....
....
....
....
....
....

DATE _____

PLACE _____

. . . .

. . . .

. . . .

. . . .

. . . .

. . . .

. . . .

. . . .

. . . .

*From whatever place I write you will expect that part of my
"Travels" will consist of excursions in my own mind.*

—SAMUEL TAYLOR COLERIDGE

. . . .

. . . .

. . . .

. . . .

. . . .

. . . .

. . . .

. . . .

. . . .

. . . .

DATE _____

PLACE _____

DATE _____

PLACE _____

DATE _____

PLACE _____

DATE _____

PLACE _____

. . . .

. . . .

. . . .

. . . .

. . . .

. . . .

. . . .

. . . .

. . . .

The aim, if reached or not, makes great the life.
Try to be Shakespeare, leave the rest to fate.

—ROBERT BROWNING

. . . .

. . . .

. . . .

. . . .

. . . .

. . . .

. . . .

. . . .

. . . .

. . . .

DATE _____

PLACE _____

....

....

....

....

....

....

....

....

....

....

....

....

....

....

....

....

....

....

....

....

....

....

DATE _____

PLACE _____

DATE _____

PLACE _____

DATE _____

PLACE _____

. . . .

. . . .

. . . .

. . . .

. . . .

. . . .

. . . .

. . . .

. . . .

If you are lucky enough to have lived in Paris as a young man, then wherever you go for the rest of your life it stays with you, for Paris is a moveable feast.

—ERNEST HEMINGWAY

. . . .

. . . .

. . . .

. . . .

. . . .

. . . .

. . . .

. . . .

. . . .

. . . .

DATE _____

PLACE _____

. . . .

. . . .

. . . .

. . . .

. . . .

. . . .

. . . .

. . . .

. . . .

. . . .

. . . .

. . . .

. . . .

. . . .

. . . .

. . . .

. . . .

. . . .

. . . .

. . . .

. . . .

. . . .

. . . .

DATE _____

PLACE _____

DATE _____

PLACE _____

DATE _____

PLACE _____

. . . .

. . . .

. . . .

. . . .

. . . .

. . . .

. . . .

. . . .

. . . .

*To withdraw myself from myself has ever been my sole,
my entire, my sincere motive for scribbling at all.*

—LORD BYRON

. . . .

. . . .

. . . .

. . . .

. . . .

. . . .

. . . .

. . . .

. . . .

. . . .

DATE

PLACE

DATE

PLACE

DATE _____

PLACE _____

DATE _____

PLACE _____

. . . .

. . . .

. . . .

. . . .

. . . .

. . . .

. . . .

. . . .

. . . .

A good rule for writers: Do not explain overmuch.

—W. SOMERSET MAUGHAM

. . . .

. . . .

. . . .

. . . .

. . . .

. . . .

. . . .

. . . .

. . . .

. . . .

DATE _____

PLACE _____

DATE _____

PLACE_____

DATE _____

PLACE _____

DATE _____

PLACE _____

. . . .

. . . .

. . . .

. . . .

. . . .

. . . .

. . . .

. . . .

. . . .

*The traveler who has gone to Italy to study the
tactile values of Giotto, or the corruption of the Papacy,
may return remembering nothing but the blue sky
and the men and women under it.*

—E. M. FORSTER, *ROOM WITH A VIEW*

. . . .

. . . .

. . . .

. . . .

. . . .

. . . .

. . . .

. . . .

. . . .

DATE _____

PLACE _____

DATE _____

PLACE _____

DATE _____

PLACE _____

. . . .

. . . .

. . . .

. . . .

. . . .

. . . .

. . . .

. . . .

. . . .

. . . .

. . . .

. . . .

. . . .

. . . .

. . . .

. . . .

. . . .

. . . .

. . . .

. . . .

. . . .

. . . .

DATE _____

PLACE _____

. . . .

. . . .

. . . .

. . . .

. . . .

. . . .

. . . .

. . . .

. . . .

I met a lot of people in Europe. I even encountered myself.

—JAMES BALDWIN

. . . .

. . . .

. . . .

. . . .

. . . .

. . . .

. . . .

. . . .

. . . .

. . . .

. . . .

DATE _____

PLACE _____

DATE _____

PLACE _____

....

....

....

....

....

....

....

....

....

....

....

....

....

....

....

....

....

....

....

....

....

....

DATE

PLACE

DATE _____

PLACE _____

. . . .

. . . .

. . . .

. . . .

. . . .

. . . .

. . . .

. . . .

. . . .

We don't receive wisdom; we must discover it for ourselves after a journey that no one can take for us or spare us.

—MARCEL PROUST

. . . .

. . . .

. . . .

. . . .

. . . .

. . . .

. . . .

. . . .

. . . .

DATE _____

PLACE _____

DATE _____

PLACE _____

....

....

....

....

....

....

....

....

....

....

....

....

....

....

....

....

....

....

....

....

....

....

DATE _____

PLACE _____

. . . .

. . . .

. . . .

. . . .

. . . .

. . . .

. . . .

. . . .

. . . .

The role of the writer is not to say what we all can say,
but what we are unable to say.

—ANAÏS NIN

. . . .

. . . .

. . . .

. . . .

. . . .

. . . .

. . . .

. . . .

. . . .

DATE _____

PLACE_____

DATE _____

PLACE _____

DATE _____

PLACE _____

. . . .

. . . .

. . . .

. . . .

. . . .

. . . .

. . . .

. . . .

. . . .

Travel, in the younger sort, is part of education;
in the elder, a part of experience.

—FRANCIS BACON

. . . .

. . . .

. . . .

. . . .

. . . .

. . . .

. . . .

. . . .

. . . .

DATE _____

PLACE _____

DATE _____

PLACE_____

....

....

....

....

....

....

....

....

....

....

....

....

....

....

....

....

....

....

....

....

....

....

DATE _____

PLACE _____

DATE _____

PLACE _____

. . . .

. . . .

. . . .

. . . .

. . . .

. . . .

. . . .

. . . .

. . . .

You must write for yourself, above all. That is (your) only hope of creating something heartfelt.

—GUSTAVE FLAUBERT

. . . .

. . . .

. . . .

. . . .

. . . .

. . . .

. . . .

. . . .

. . . .

DATE _____

PLACE _____

DATE

PLACE

DATE

PLACE

DATE _____

PLACE _____

....

....

....

....

....

....

....

....

....

We travel, some of us forever, to seek other states,
other lives, other souls.

—ANAÏS NIN

....

....

....

....

....

....

....

....

....

....

DATE _____

PLACE _____

DATE _____

PLACE _____

DATE

PLACE

DATE _____

PLACE _____

. . . .

. . . .

. . . .

. . . .

. . . .

. . . .

. . . .

. . . .

. . . .

The writer is committed when he plunges to the very
depths of himself with the intent to disclose,
not his individuality, but his person in the complex
society that conditions and supports him.

—JEAN PAUL SARTRE

. . . .

. . . .

. . . .

. . . .

. . . .

. . . .

. . . .

. . . .

DATE _____

PLACE _____

DATE _____

PLACE _____

....
....
....
....
....
....
....
....
....
....
....
....
....
....
....
....
....
....
....
....
....
....
....

GENERAL RECOMMENDATIONS
───⟶ FOR TRAVELERS ⟵───

TRAVEL LIGHT

This is a sure way to have a better trip. The extra planning it takes to travel with a light load is well worth the effort. Here are some things to keep in mind.

* You do not need to carry more luggage for a three-month trip than for a three-week trip.

* A bag with the dimensions 9 x 22 x 14 inches will fit under most airplane seats.

* Select clothes that will wash easily, resist wrinkling, and take up little space in your suitcase. Choose colors that make all your clothes interchangeable.

LANGUAGE

Consider taking a language class or hiring a tutor if you're going to spend much time in one country. Make a point of learning some of the language of the country you'll be visiting no matter how short your stay. Travel writer Deborah Burns recommends learning the following foreign language basis:

* Polite words, e.g., "hello," "please," "thank you," "excuse me," and "good-bye."

* The personal pronoun "you" in its different forms (formal and informal usage).

* Verbs "to be," "to go," and "to have" and their tenses.

* How to say "Where is ...?"

* Emergency words, e.g., "I need a doctor," "Help!" and "Where is the toilet?"

* Add five additional words to your foreign language vocabulary each day.

PERSONAL SAFETY AND SECURITY

There are ways to minimize the threat of theft, but also consider minimizing the effect that theft, should it happen, can have on your trip.

* Simply leave all valuables and items of strong sentimental value at home.
* Keep all essentials, e.g., passport and credit cards, in a money bag or pouch on your person.
* Consider buying an inexpensive camera.
* Divide cash you are carrying on your person between your wallet and your money belt.

FRESH PERSPECTIVE

* Seek out the local shopping haunts, read the local newspapers (if in a language you know), and walk through neighborhoods that are off the tourist path.
* Beat the crowds by spending the night at popular day-trip destinations found near major resorts and large cities.
* Get up and out at first light. The early morning hours can offer a peaceful, personal view outdoors.
* Go late to museums and other tourist attractions. The last few hours can be the least crowded.
* Avoid the weekly free days at museums during busy tourist seasons. These can be a bad bargain when long lines and overcrowding are part of the deal.

NOTE THE FOLLOWING ADVICE FROM THE STATE DEPARTMENT:

* Make sure you have a signed, valid passport and that you have filled in the emergency information page before you leave. Leave your passport number with someone back home and have their phone number memorized.
* Familiarize yourself with local laws and customs. Remember that the U.S. Constitution does not follow you-you are subject to the laws of a foreign country while you are there.

* Leave your itinerary with family or friends so that you can be contacted in an emergency.
* Do not accept packages from strangers or leave your luggage in unattended areas.
* Avoid violating local laws by dealing only with authorized agents when purchasing art, antiques, or when you are exchanging money.
* If you get into trouble, contact the U.S. consul.

HEALTH AND WELL-BEING ON THE ROAD

The health precautions advisable for travel to Western Europe are essentially the same as those recommended in the U.S. Even so, don't ignore the advice. Travel and illness are an unpleasant combination.

Before you leave on your trip, review the Center for Disease Control's recommendations at www.cdc.gov/travel, or reference the health considerations for specific cities and good general guidelines at Kroll Travel Watch (www.kroll-worldwide.com).

Bring along a basic medical kit containing aspirin/acetaminophen, antibiotics, rehydration salts, insect repellent, antihistamines, motion sickness preventative, and sunscreen.

The International Association for Medical Assistance to Travelers advises travelers of health risks, and makes medical care available to travelers by English or French-speaking doctors. Membership is free: IAMAT (www.sentex.net/~iamat), 417 Center St., Lewiston, NY 14092.

TRAVEL INSURANCE

Determine what coverage you already have. Note that:
* Homeowners' and renters' policies may include liability or baggage/personal property protection for travelers
* Health insurance policies often offer some coverage for travelers
* Auto insurance may cover rental-car use
* Life insurance policies usually cover accidental death or injury

* Credit cards sometimes offer travel protection, such as loss/damage waiver for car rental, or flight change/cancellation coverage.

Consider purchasing a trip cancellation/interruption insurance policy that includes medical transportation and evacuation. These policies are generally the most cost-effective and often cover losses not covered by a person's existing insurance.

Emergency assistance insurance gives you money on the spot to cover emergency situations. When investigating this type of insurance, ask if a 24-hour service is available to call for immediate help. The following well-established emergency assistance providers are a good starting point for comparison shopping:

American Express Global Assist Service
(www.travel.americanexpress.com/travel)
Phone: U.S.: 800-554-AMEX; abroad (call collect): 202-783-7474

International SOS Assistance, Inc.
(www.aeaintl.com/medical.htm)
Phone: 215-244-1500

Assist Card
(www.assist-card.com)
Phone: 800-874-2223

Examine policy exclusions under a microscope. Most travel insurance policies contain liberal exclusions. Don't wait until making a claim to learn about them.

Be sure to pack (1) your insurance card, (2) a claim form from your insurer (this will facilitate reimbursement), (3) your insurance company's phone number, and (4) your agent's name and phone number.

Getting Around

RAIL

Travel by rail is a wonderful way to meet Europeans and traveling Americans like yourself. In Europe, trains are clean, run on time, and are the most popular means of inter-urban travel. With sleeper cars or couchettes, trains can also provide very inexpensive overnight accommodations. If you need to get somewhere in a hurry, very high speed trains like the French TGV (Trés Grande Vitesse) travel at speeds in excess of 160 miles per hour, and depart and arrive at city center train stations.

For American and Canadian travelers, Eurail passes provide an inexpensive means of rail travel in Europe. There are many different passes—Eurail Sixteen Country, Britrail, Youth, Single Country; two-week, three-week, or more; Mixed Use rail and rental car; metro passes for cities like London and Paris—with many different restrictions. All passes must be bought in the U.S. before traveling abroad!

A Eurail pass give you unlimited first-class travel in Austria, Belgium, Denmark, Finland, France, Germany, Greece, Hungary, Ireland, Italy, Luxembourg, the Netherlands, Norway, Portugal, Spain, Sweden, and Switzerland.

When traveling by rail, remember the following:

* Some trains (like the TGV, Eurostar) require monetary supplements even if you use your Eurail pass. Information on the Eurail pass (www.raileurope.com) and other European rail passes can be found at Europrail International (www.odyssey.on.ca/~europrail). This site includes fares, schedules of popular routes, how to purchase rail passes, and a terrific interactive rail map. Or see a travel agent.

* Cities have more than one train station, so be clear about arriving and departure stations.

* Couchettes and sleepers must be reserved.

* If you plan on extensive travel in Europe, invest in a Thomas Cook European Timetable to plan your itinerary. This publication, updated monthly, offers a complete listing of train schedules and advises when supplements or reservations are necessary. Available through the Thomas Cook Web site (www.ThomasCook.com) or Rail Europe Inc., c/o Forsyth Travel Inc., 226 Westchester Ave., White Plains, NY 10604, fax: (914) 681-7251.

* Obtain the national timetable(s) published by the state railroad(s) if you intend to travel by train through just a few countries. Information can be found in The European Planning & Rail Guide, 1557 Mead Court, Ann Arbor, MI 48105-1304, phone: (734) 668-0529 fax: (734) 665-5986.

* Book Recommendation: *Europe by Train 1999—The Number One Guide to Budget Travel* by Katie Wood. This book marries a complete rail travel resource with an excellent guide to the basics of budget travel.

* Students and seniors can obtain special discounts on rail travel through membership in organizations such as Hostelling International (www.iyhf.org), the Council on International Educational Exchange (CIEE) (www.ciee.org), or www.hostels.com. Find phone numbers on the Web site.

Auto

Automobile travel advantages include room for extra gear, freedom from public transportation timetables, cheaper group travel, and the access to picnic sites that the car allows. For information:

* Car rental guidelines and reservations: Travelocity (www.travelocity.com) and Budget Rent-a-Car On-line (www.budgetrentacar.com). Note: As with rail passes, car rentals are significantly cheaper when pre-booked.

* Drive in all Western European countries (except Spain) with a U.S. driver's license. Spain (and many countries outside Western Europe) require travelers to have an

International Driver's Permit. This can be obtained through the American Automobile Association (www.aaa.com).

* Utilize MapQuest's Interaction Driving Directions (www.mapquest.com). Just plug in an address to generate street map and directions.

BOAT

Traveling by boat is an unmatched way to look at Europe from another perspective. Trips on Europe's large rivers and lakes are scenic, relaxing, and memorable—but they are not quick or cheap. (Rail-pass holders get various boating discounts.) Voyages can be taken on many inland waterways via steamer or barge.

There are more boat trip choices in the summer months. Between June and September for example, you can cruise from Amsterdam to Vienna via the Main-Danube Canal, which was built to connect the Danube and the Rhine rivers.

The Forsyth Travel Library's Ferries, Steamers, Boats and Railroad Bonuses Web page (www.forsyth.com) offers a great breakdown of boating routes and itineraries.

FERRY

There is quite a bit of competition in the European ferry boat market. This creates a lot of choices, but figuring out your itinerary can get complicated.

* The best deals are usually obtained by booking ahead.

* The Mining Co.'s European Ferries web page (www.goeurope.miningco.com) is the place to start researching ferry routes. This page has links to ferry lines serving the English Channel/Irish Sea and Northern/Southern Europe.

* The Thomas Cook guide to Greek Island Hopping (www.ThomasCook.com) is an essential resource with ferry times, routes, and tourist information. Extremely thorough, but restricted to the maze of boat routes throughout the Greek islands.

Touring Europe by bicycle is eminently doable even if you are not a serious athlete. When planning a cycling itinerary, remember:

* Don't plan too strenuous an agenda. One of the best parts of cycling in a foreign country is the opportunity to meet the people who live there. (An experienced cyclist can average 80 km/day.)

* Michelin maps are particularly useful because they indicate scenic routes.

* Bring a bike helmet, a good lock (and use it), a puncture-repair kit, extra inner tubes, and a pannier to balance your belongings on either side of the bike frame.

* If you plan to take your own bike, check with the airline before you travel. A partial dismantling of the bike might be necessary before you box it (pick up a discarded box from a local bike shop). Minimum is taking off the pedals, and front tire, and loosening the handlebars and turning them parallel to the frame. A small piece of wood secured between the front forks after the tire is removed can save the forks from being bent if the airline mishandles the box. Before boxing deflate the tires.

* Consider taking the train for the difficult or less scenic portions of your trip. Some trains handle bikes as luggage for a small fee. On other trains you must register your bike for shipping, possibly on another train. In England on the local trains, a bicyclist merely jumps on the rail car (usually the last car). The bike stays with the mail bags and the bicyclist walks through to the next car to take a seat. It's sometimes possible to take the wheels off and transport your bike as hand luggage.

The Cyclists' Touring Club (www.ctc.org.uk) of the U.K. can help with information about train transport, as well as detailed routes, suggested itineraries, maps, and even insurance. Phone: 483-417217.

* Check out the guided bike tour option with companies such as Hiking and Biking Guided Adventures for Europe (www.andiamoadventours.com).

Bus

Buses are not as much fun, certainly less comfortable, and generally slower than trains, but they do have the advantage of being cheaper.

* A Web site called Backpack Europe (www.backpackeurope.com/howtotravel.html) makes an impassioned case for the budgetary value of going "coach" through Europe, and includes price comparisons, basic bus-related links, and route particulars.

* Eurolines (www.eurolines.co.uk) is Europe's largest network of international buses. Look into the National Express Discount Coachcard options for impressive savings.

* Busabout (www.busabout.com) is targeting the youth market by promoting an unlimited "hop-on, hop-off" coach pass and a program called "Bedabout" featuring inexpensive accommodations throughout Europe.

U.S. EMBASSIES AND
——— CONSULATES   ———

I am carrying out my plan, so long formulated, of keeping a journal. What I most keenly wish is not to forget that I am writing for myself alone. Thus I shall improve myself. These pages will reproach me for my changes of mind.

—EUGENE DELACROIX

U.S. Consular officers assist American citizens in everything from replacing lost passports to emergency evacuations, birth and death registrations, and adoption assistance. Should you be arrested, however, the consulate is generally limited to visiting you in jail and notifying your family. Also, note that travel warnings are reactive, i.e., a warning is issued after something dangerous happens. It's in your best interest to learn all you can about the places you're going, and, once there, practice vigilance.

BUREAU OF CONSULAR AFFAIRS (WWW.TRAVEL.STATE.GOV)
This home page links you to a wealth of information about required travel documents, travel safety, and the consular services available to Americans abroad.

Go directly to "Links to U.S. Embassies and Consulates Worldwide" (www.travel.state.gov/links.html) to access the home page of the embassy in the country you're visiting.

COUNTRY	ADDRESS	PHONE
Austria	9 Boltzmanngasse 16, Vienna	(0222-313-39)
Belgium	Blvd. Due Regent 27, ß-1000 Brussels	(513-38-30)
Czech Republic /Trziste	15, 118 01 Praha 1, Prague	(420-2) 5753-0663

continued on page 140

Denmark	Dag Hammarskjolds Alle 24 Copenhagen	(31-42-31-44)
England	24 Grosvenor Square, London, WI	(0171-499-9000)
Finland	Hainen Puistotie 14A Helsinki	(0717-19-31)
France	2 rue Saint-Florentin, 75382 Paris Cedex	(08 01-43-12-48-40)
Germany	Clayallee 170, 14195 Berlin	(228-3391)
Greece	Leoforos Vasillissis Sofias Blvd., Athens	(668-721-2951)
Hungary	Szabadság tév 12., H-1054 Budapest	(475-4400)
Ireland	42 Elgin Rd., Ballsbridge, Dublin	(353-1-668-8777)
Italy	Via Vittorio Veneto 119/A, Rome	(46-741)
Netherlands	Lange Voorhout 102, The Hague	(70-351-4111)
Norway	Drammensveien	18 0244 1510 22448550
Poland	Al. Ujazdowakie 29131 00-540 Warsaw	(48-221628-3041)
Portugal	Avenida das Forcas Armadas, Lisbon	(1-347-4892)
Spain	Calle Serrano 75, Madrid	(577-4000)
Sweden	Dag Hammarskjölds Vag 31, SE 115 89 Stockholm	(08-78353 00)
Switzerland	1-3 Ave. de la Paix, Geneva, Jubilaeumsrasse 93 (31-357-70-11)	(738-76-13)
Turkey	110 Ataturk Blvd., (41) 468-6110 Ankara	

━━ꞔ Keeping in Touch ꞔ━━

The diary is an art form just as much as the novel or the play. The diary simply requires a greater canvas.

—Henry Miller

E-MAIL

Keeping in touch with home, friends, and family while traveling is easier than ever with the advent of the Internet. E-mail offers the middle ground between the immediacy of the telephone and the thoughtfulness of the written word.

E-mail is also an excellent way to keep in touch with people you meet in Europe while you're still on the road. Whether fellow travelers or locals, as long as they have access to the Net, you can stay in contact. In addition, you can send an email out to multiple recipients, saving you money and time.

Whether you're bringing along a portable computer or utilizing the increasingly popular cybercafes, there are a few things to keep in mind.

Cybercafes

* Cybercafes can be found primarily in the larger cities of Europe. Be sure to check online guides such as The Net Café Guide (www.netcafeguide.com) for an updated list.

* You can access your e-mail account from any computer linked to the Internet as long as it runs some kind of email software. In order to access your Internet mail account be sure to have on hand: (1) your incoming (POP or IMAP) server name, (2) your account name, and (3) your password. You can get this information from your ISP (Internet Service Provider) or network manager.

* You can also pick up mail via cybercafes by opening a Web-based e-mail account such as Hotmail (www.hotmail.com). You can then access your e-mail from any

computer connected to the Internet, running a standard Web browser.

* Be aware: the cybercafes vary in quality, ambiance, and price. Most charge for computer use by the hour, and the fees range from fairly reasonable to quite cheap. Remember that all computer connections are not created equal, so expect variety.

PORTABLE COMPUTERS

Be sure to buy the following before you leave home:

* an AC adapter to protect your computer from power-supply variance.

* a plug adapter for each country you'll be traveling in.

* a reliable global modem (you can't tell if your PC-card model will work in another country until you get there).

* a US RJ-11 telephone adapter that works with your modem.

TELEPHONES

There are a variety of ways to communicate and stay in touch by telephone, but first, here are a few general guidelines:

* Make a point of familiarizing yourself with the pay phones of the country you're visiting before you actually need to make a call.

* Consider getting a good international plan with your long-distance provider at home and having your family call you.

* Note that many foreign telephone directories have a page in English that will list the number of a multilingual operator.

PHONE CARDS

Purchasing local phone cards—the prepaid ones sold in the country you're visiting—is an easy and cost-efficient way to go. These cards are a boon to staying within a budget. On the downside, the time limitation on prepaid phone cards can at times be annoying and inconvenient.

CALLING CARDS

Calling cards issued by long-distance service providers are easy to use and affordable, but generally not as inexpensive as prepaid phone cards.

REVERSE CHARGES

Be wary about calling collect, as the cost for convenience can be exorbitant.

SENDING/RECEIVING MAIL AND PACKAGES

* General Delivery or Poste Restante: You can receive mail at most foreign post offices. Generally your mail will be held for 30 days if not picked up. You'll need to show your passport to pick up your mail.
* American Express offices are also good places to receive mail. You can utilize this service if you carry an American Express credit card or if you've purchased American Express traveler's checks.
* Federal Express (www.FedEx.com) and United Parcel Service (www.ups.com) are two more options for sending and receiving packages. You can get information for the country you're visiting at the above Web sites.

MAJOR CITIES

AMSTERDAM
Airport: Schiphol (18 km. Southwest)
Bookstore: American Book Centre, Ph: 625-55-37, Kalverstraat 185.
Cybercafe: In de Waag, Ph. 422-77-72, basement of the
  500-year-old Waag building on Nieuwmarket.
Tourist info: VVV Tourist Office, Ph. 0-900-404-
  04-00, Stationsplien 10 (in the Old Dutch Coffeehouse).
ATHENS
Airport: Hellinikon (7 mi.)
Bookstore: Elefheroudakis. Two branches: Panepistimiou 17 and
  Nikis 4.
Cybercafe: Cybercave at the Student & Traveller's Inn,
  Kydathineon 16.

BUDAPEST

Airport: Ferihegy II

Bookstores: Bestsellers, Ph. 312-1295, V Oktober 6 Utea 11, M3 Arany Janos Utea.

Cybercafe: Plaza Internet Club and Cybercafe, Ph: 465-1126, Duna Plaza Shopping Center, XIII, Vaci Ut 178.

Tourist Info: Tour Inform, Ph: 117-9800, V Suto Utea 2, M1, M2, M3 Deak ter/tram 47, 49.

COPENHAGEN

Airport: Copenhagen

Bookstores: GAD, Stroget at Vimmelskaftet 32; Arnold Busck, Kobmagergade 49.

Cybercafes: Babel, Ph. 45-33-33-93-38, Frederiksborggade 33; NetPoint Royal, Ph: 45-70-22-10-08, Hammerichsgade 3.

Tourist Info: Tourist Office, Bernstorffsgade 1, DK-1577, Copenhagen V, www.dt.dk.

HELSKINKI

Airport: Helsinki/Vantaa

Bookstore: The American Bookshop Ph: 358-9-441-901, Muse. Katu 3.

Cybercafes: Vanha, Mannerheimintie 3.

Tourist Info: City of Helsinki Tourist Office, Ph: 358-9-169-3757, Pohjoiseplanadi 19.

ISTANBUL

Airport: Atatürk

Bookstores: Remzi Kitaberi, Ph. 234-5475, Rumeli Caddesi 44, Nisantasi; Galeri Kayseri, Ph: 512-0456, Divan Yolu 38, Sultanahamet.

Cybercafes: Yagmur Cybercafe, Ph: 292-3020, 1812 Seyhbender Sok. Asmalimescit Beyoglu, www.citlembik.com.tr.

Tourist Info: Atatürk Airport Tourist Center, Ph. 212-663-0704.

LONDON

Airports: Heathrow; Gatwick

Bookstores (two of many): Daunt Books, Ph. 0171-224-2295, 83 Marylebone High St. W1; Foyles, Ph: 0171-437-5560, 119 Charing Cross Rd. WC2.

Cybercafe: Cyberia Café, Ph: 0171-209-0982, 39 Whitfield St. W1; New Broadway W5.

Tourist Info: London Tourist Information Center, Ph: 0171-730-3488, Victoria Station; Forecourt; British Travel Centre, 12 Regent St., Piccadilly Circus, SW1.

MADRID

Airport: Barajas Airport

Bookstores: The International Bookshop, Ph. 91-541-7291. Génova 3; Turner's English Bookshop, Ph. 91-319-0926.

Cybercafe: La Casa de Internet, Calle de Luchana 20 (metro Bilboa).

Tourist Info: Main Tourist Office, Ph: 91-429-49-51, Calle de Duquede Medinaceli 2

OSLO

Airport: Fornebu

Bookstore: Tanum Libris, Ph: 22-41-22-00, Karl Johans Gate 37-41.

Cybercafe: Studenten, Ph: 22-46-56-80, Karl Johans Gate 45, www.studenten-café.no.

Tourist info: Norway Info Center, Ph: 22-83-00-50, Old Vestbanen Railway Station.

PARIS

Airports: Charles de Gaulle Airport, aka Roissy; Orly Airport

Bookstores: Shakespeare & Co., Ph: 01-43-26-96-50, 37 Rue de la Bûchere; WH Smith, Ph: 01-44-77-88-99, 248 Rue de Rivoli.

Cybercafes: The Web Bar, Ph. 01-42-72-66-55, 32 Rue de Picardie (www.webbar.fr); Café Orbital, Ph: 01 43-25-76-77, 13 Rue de Médicis.

Tourist info: Paris Tourist office, Ph. 01-49-52-53-54; 01-49-52-53-56 (recorded info in English), 127 av. Des. Champs-Elysées.

PRAGUE

Airport: Ruzneÿ

Bookstores: The Globe Bookstore, Ph: 6671 2610, Janovskeho 14, Prague 2; Big Ben Book Shop, Ph: 232 8249, Rybna 2, Prague 1.

Cybercafes: Netwave Internet , Ph. 420 (0) 2 9618 6600, 8 Na Bojisti, www.netwave.cz; PI@neta, Ph: 420 (0) 2673 1182, 102 Vinohradska St., www.planeta.cz.

Tourist info: Prague Tourist Center, Ph. 2421 2209, Praha 1, Rytirska 12.

ROME

Airport: Leonardo da Vinci

Bookstores: The Corner Bookshop, Ph: 583 69 42, Via del Moro, Trastavere; Anglo-American Bookstore, Ph: 06-6795222, Via della Vite 102.

Cybercafe: Explorer Café, Ph: 324-17-57, Via dei Gracchi 85 (near the Vatican).

Tourist info: EPT (Rome Provincial Tourist), Ph. 06-48-89-92-53, three locations: Via Pariggi 5,00185; Termini Station; Fiumicino Airport.

STOCKHOLM

Airport: Arlanda Airport

Bookstore: English Book Center, Ph: 08-30-14-47, Surbrunnsgatan 51, www.engbookeen.se.

Cybercafe: Nine Studios, Ph: 86-12-90-09, 44 Odengatan, www.nine.nu.

Tourist Info: Tourist Center, Ph. 08-789-24-90, Hamngatan 27.

VIENNA

Airport: Schwechat

Bookstores: The British Bookshop, Ph: 512-19-45, Weihburggasse, 24-6; Shakespeare & Co. Booksellers, Ph: 535-50-53, Sterngasse 2.

Cybercafes: Café Stein, Ph: 319-72-411, Währinger Strasse 6; Virgin Megastore, Ph: 581-05-00, Mariahilfer Strasse 37-39.

Tourist info: City Tourist Office, Kärntnerstr. 38 (behind the Staatsoper).

WARSAW

Airport: Warsaw International

Bookstores: American Bookstore, Ph: 8-26-01-61, Ul. Krakowskie, Przedmiescie 45; Traveller's Shop, Ph. 658-46-26, Ul. Kaliska 8/10.

Cybercafe: Planet 808 Internet Club, Ph. 48-22-828-9107, 2 Krolewska St., www.planet.808.ii.pl.

Tourist Info: Tourist Info Center, Ph. 635-18-81, Plac Zamkowy 1/3.

ZURICH

Airport: Zurich-Kloten Bookstores: Stäheli English Bookshop, Ph: 201-33-02, Bahnhofstrasse 70; Librairie Poyot, Bahnhofstrasse 9.

Bookstore: Stäheli English Bookshop, Ph. 201-33-02, Bahnhofstrasse 70.

Cybercafe: Cybergate, in the main hall of the train station (www.cybergate.ibm.ch).

Tourist Info: Tourist Service, in the main hall of the train station, Ph. 215-40-00 (www.zurichtourism.ch).

TELEPHONE CODES

COUNTRY	COUNTRY CODE	OPERATOR
Austria	43	00
Belgium	32	00
Czech Republic	42	00
Denmark	45	00
Finland	358	990
France	33	00 (wait for tone)
Hungary	36	00
Ireland	353	00
Italy	39	00
Netherlands	31	00
Norway	47	095
Poland	48	00
Portugal	351	00
Spain	34	00 (wait for tone)
Sweden	46	009 (wait for tone)
Switzerland	41	00
Turkey	90	00
U.K.	44	00

EUROPEAN HOLIDAYS

The following guide to holidays can be used as an aid to European travel planning. More detailed information, especially about floating holidays, can be found at Go-Global (www.aglobalworld.com).

AUSTRIA

1/1, New Year's Day; 1/6, Epiphany; 5/1, Labor Day; 8/15, Assumption of the Blessed Virgin Mary; 10/26, National Day; 11/1, All Saints Day; 12/8, Immaculate Conception; 12/25, Christmas Day; 12/26, Boxing Day.

BELGIUM

1/1, New Year's Day; 5/1, Labor Day; 7/1, Flemish Community Holiday (the date of the Guldensporenslag, a battle in 1302 where the Flemish asserted their independence from France); 7/21, National Holiday; 8/15, Assumption of the Blessed Virgin Mary; 9/27, French Community Holiday; 11/1, All Saints Day; 11/11, Armistice Day; 12/25, Christmas Day.

CZECH REPUBLIC

1/1, New Year's Day; 5/1, May Day; 5/8, Liberation Day; 7/5, St. Cyril and St. Methodius; 7/6, Jan Hus; 10/28, Establishment of Independent Czechoslovakia; 12/24, Christmas Eve; 12/25, Christmas Day; 12/26, Second Day of Christmas.

DENMARK

1/1, New Year's Day; 6/5, Constitution Day; 12/2, Christmas Eve; 12/25, Christmas; 12/26, Boxing Day; 12/31, New Year's Eve.

FINLAND

1/1, New Year's Day; 1/6, Epiphany; 5/1, May Day or Vappu; 11/1, All Saints Day; 2nd Sunday in November, Father's Day; 12/6, Independence Day; 12/24, Christmas Eve;12/25, Christmas Day; 12/26, Second Day of Christmas.

FRANCE

1/1, New Year's Day; 5/1, Labor Day; 5/8, Fete de la Victoire 1945 (WW II Victory Day); 7/13, Bank Holiday; 7/14, Bastille Day; 8/15, Assumption of the Blessed Virgin Mary; 11/1, All Saints Day; 11/11, Armistice Day; 12/25, Christmas Day; 12/26, Second Day of Christmas (in Alsace Lorraine only).

GERMANY

1/1, New Year's Day; 1/6, Epiphany-in BadenWÿrttemberg, Bavaria, and Saxony-Anhalt; 5/1, May Day or Labor Day; 8/15, Assumption of the Blessed Virgin Mary-in Bavaria (in predominantly Catholic communities) and Saarland only; 10/3, Day of German Unity; 10/31, Reformation Day-in Brandenburg, Mecklenburg-Vorpommern, Saxony, Saxony-Anhalt and Thuringia (predominantly Evangelical communities) only; 11/1, All Saints Day-in Baden-Wÿrttemberg, Bavaria, North Rhine-Westphalia, Rhineland Palatinate, Saarland, and Thuringia (predominantly Catholic communities) only; 12/24, Christmas Eve-Government closed, half day for shops; 12/25, Christmas Day; Dec. 26, Second Day of Christmas; 12/31, New Year's Eve.

GREECE

1/1, New Year's Day; 1/6, Epiphany; 3/25, Greek Independence Day; 5/1, May Day; 8/15, Assumption of the Blessed Virgin Mary; 10/28, Ochi Day; 12/25, Christmas Day; 12/26, Second Day of Christmas.

HUNGARY

1/1, New Year's Day; 3/15, National Day; 5/1, Labor Day; 8/20, Constitution Day; 10/23, Republic Day; 12/25, Christmas; 12/26, Boxing Day.

REPUBLIC OF IRELAND

1/1, New Year's Day; 3/17, St. Patrick's Day*; 1st Monday in May, Bank Holiday; 1st Monday in June, Bank Holiday; 1st Monday in August, Bank Holiday; Last Monday in October, Summer Bank Holiday; 12/25, Christmas Day; 12/26, Boxing Day.

*St. Patrick's Day is moved to the Monday following if it falls on a Sunday.

ITALY

1/1, New Year's Day; 1/6, Epiphany; 4/25, Liberation Day; 5/1, May Day; Sunday nearest June 2, Anniversary of the Republic; 8/15, Assumption of the Blessed Virgin Mary; 11/1, All Saint's Day; Sunday nearest 4 November, World War I Victory Anniversary Day; 12/8, Immaculate Conception; 12/25, Christmas Day; 12/26, Boxing Day or St. Stephen's Day.

LUXEMBOURG

1/1, New Year's Day; 5/1, May Day; 6/23, National Day (Sovereign's Birthday)*; 8/15, Assumption of the Blessed Virgin Mary; 9/1, Luxembourg City Kermesse (City of Luxembourg only); 11/1, All Saints Day; 12/25, Christmas Day; 12/26, St. Stephen's Day.

*National Day (the Grand Duke's Birthday) is transferred to a Monday if it falls on a Sunday.

MONACO

1/1, New Year's Day; 2/26-27, Sainte-Devote Day; 5/1, Labor Day; 8/15, Assumption of the Blessed Virgin Mary (Government employees only); 11/1, All Saints Day; 11/18-19, National Day; 12/8, Immaculate Conception; 12/24, Christmas Eve; 12/25, Christmas Day; 12/31, New Year's Eve.

NETHERLANDS

1/1, New Year's Day; 4/30, Queen's Day; 12/25, Christmas Day; 12/26, Boxing Day.

NORWAY

1/2, New Year's Day; 5/1, May Day; 5/17, National Independence Day; 12/24, Christmas Eve; 12/25, Christmas; 12/26, Boxing Day; 12/31, New Year's Eve (1/2 day from noon).

POLAND

1/1, New Year's Day; 5/1, May Day; 5/3, Constitution Day; 8/15, Assumption of the Blessed Virgin Mary; 11/1,

All Saints Day; 11/11, Independence Day; 12/25, Christmas Day; 12/26, Second Day of Christmas.

PORTUGAL

1/1, New Year's Day; 4/25, Liberation Day; 5/1, Labor Day; 6/10, National Day; 8/15, Assumption of the Blessed Virgin Mary; 10/5, Republic Day; 11/1, All Saints Day; 12/1, Independence Day; 12/8, Immaculate Conception; 12/24, Christmas Eve; 12/25, Christmas Day. Local Fiestas: Portugal has a remarkable number of festivals and local holidays, including the Holy Week Festival (Braga; Easter), which features colorful processions; the Festas de Saõ (Oporto; 24 June), when everyone dances through the streets, amicably hitting each other over the head with leeks; and the Feira de Martinho Goleg; November), which showcases all manner of horses, riding contests and bullfights. The following are known dates: 5/18, Municipal Holiday (Ponta Delgado); 6/1, Regional holiday (Azores); 6/13, Saint Anthony's Day (Lisbon); 6/24, Municipal holiday (Oporto); 7/1, Regional holiday (Madeira); 8/21, Municipal holiday (Funchal); 12/26, Boxing Day (Madeira).

SPAIN

1/1, New Year's Day; 1/6, Epiphany; 2/28, Day of Andalucia (Andalucia only); 5/1, May Day/Labor Day; 7/25, National day of Galicia (Galicia only); 8/15, Feast of the Assumption; 9/11, National Day of Catalonia (Catalonia only); 10/12, Spanish National Day; 11/1, All Saints Day; 12/6, Day of the Constitution; 12/8, Immaculate Conception; 12/25 Christmas Day.

SWEDEN

1/1 New Year's Day; 1/6, Epiphany; 6/6, National Day; 12/25, Christmas; 12/26 Boxing Day.

SWITZERLAND

1/1, New Year's Day; 1/2, Berchtold's Day; 8/1, National Day; 12/25, Christmas Day; 26 December, St. Stephen's Day.

TURKEY

1/1, New Year's Day; 4/23, National Sovereignty and Children's Day; 5/19 Ataturk Commemorative Day; 8/30, Victory Day; 10/29, Republic Day.

UNITED KINGDOM OF GREAT BRITAIN AND NORTHERN IRELAND

(The following are holidays throughout the United Kingdom unless otherwise specified) 1/1, New Year's Day; 1/2, Bank holiday (Scotland only); 3/17, St. Patrick's Day (N. Ireland only); 1st Monday in May, May Day; Last Monday in May, Bank Holiday; 7/12, Battle of the Boyne Day (N. Ireland only); First Monday in August, Summer Bank Holiday (Scotland only); Last Monday in August, Summer Bank Holiday (except Scotland); 12/25, Christmas Day; 12/26, Boxing Day. Holidays falling on a weekend are celebrated on the Monday following.

Returning
——⁊ to the U.S. ⁊——

It is a strange thing to come home while yet on the journey. You cannot at all realize how strange it will be.

—Selma Lagellot

* The Immigration and Naturalization Service monitors the flow of people entering the U.S. If you reenter the U.S. by plane, you pass through Immigration before picking up your baggage, and then you proceed through customs. U.S. citizens have the right to reenter the U.S. without a visa or other papers, but you may be asked questions about the nature of your travels. The best plan for keeping this process brief is to respond with accuracy and patience. The Customs Service regulates items entering the U.S. and makes sure that all duties and taxes are paid on imported items.

* As a U.S. resident your duty-free exemption is $400, meaning that you can buy up to $400 worth of goods and not have to pay a tax on it. You are required to declare anything you have acquired during your travels, including gifts, on the Customs Declaration Form and assign a total value. Based on your declaration and the judgment of the customs officer, your baggage or your person may be searched. Customs officials do not have to show probable cause for a search.

* If you are in doubt about whether or not an item should be declared, declare it. A mistake may net you the duty fee or tax, but stiff fines or penalties can be levied, and more serious oversights can be criminally prosecuted.

* Although it is uncommon for a Customs search to be more than a quick look in a couple of bags, it's legal for Customs officers to look through financial records and other person-al effects, dismantle luggage, or cause you to miss a con-necting flight. Be prepared to prove that your personal belongings were yours prior to departure. You can register items that have serial numbers with the Customs Service before you leave. For valuable items that lack serial num-bers, such as jewelry, consider bringing receipts, appraisals, or insurance papers to show ownership.

* Learn more about U.S. Customs rules, your personal exemption, restricted or prohibited merchandise, etc., by checking out "Traveler Information" at the U.S. Customs Web site (www.customs.ustreas.gov/travel).

Conversion Charts

WEIGHT

1 ounce = 28.3 grams

1 gram = .035 ounce

1 pound = .454 kilogram

1 kilogram = 2.2 pounds

VOLUME

1 mile = 1.61 kilometers

1 pint = .571 liter

1 kilometer = .62 mile

1 liter = 1.76 pints

LENGTH/DISTANCE

1 inch = 2.54 centimeters

1 centimeter = .394 inch

1 foot = .3 meter

1 meter = 3.28 feet

TEMPERATURE

°F	-40	32	41	50	59	68	86	100	104
°C	-40	0	5	10	15	20	30	38	40

VOLTAGES AND PLUGS

There is a wide variation in voltages and plug configuration worldwide; here are some regional standards.

   North America–110 volts

   Asia–220 volts

   United Kingdom–220 volts (three pin plug)

   Continental Europe–240 volts (three pin plug)

CLOTHING SIZES

WOMEN'S CLOTHING

Dresses, Suits, Coats, Sweaters, etc.

Canada/US	4	6	8	10	12	14	16	18
UK	6	8	10	12	14	16	18	20
Europe	32	34	36	38	40	42	44	46

WOMEN'S SHOES

Canada/US	$5^1/_2$	6	$6^1/_2$	7	$7^1/_2$	8	$8^1/_2$	9	$9^1/_2$	10
UK	4	$4^1/_2$	5	$5^1/_2$	6	$6^1/_2$	7	$7^1/_2$	8	$8^1/_2$
Europe	37	38	39	40	41					

MEN'S CLOTHING

Suits, Jackets, Sweaters, etc.

Europe	44	46	48	$49^1/_2$	51	$52^1/_2$	54	$55^1/_2$	57
Canada /US/UK	34	35	36	37	38	39	40	41	42

MEN'S SHOES

Canada/US	8	$8^1/_2$	9	$9^1/_2$	10	$10^1/_2$	11
UK	$7^1/_2$	8	$8^1/_2$	9	$9^1/_2$	10	$10^1/_2$
Europe	41	42	43	43	44	44	45

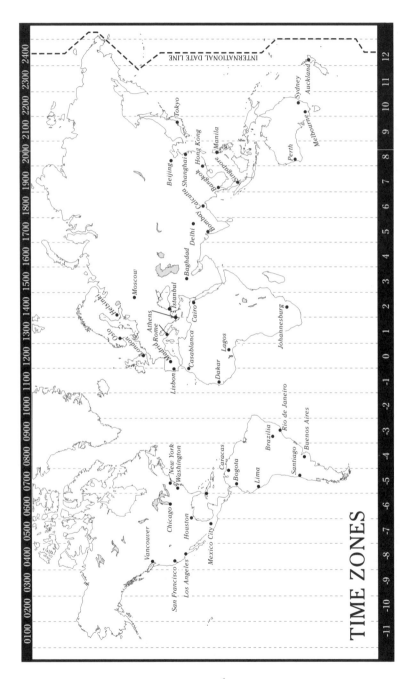

TIME ZONES

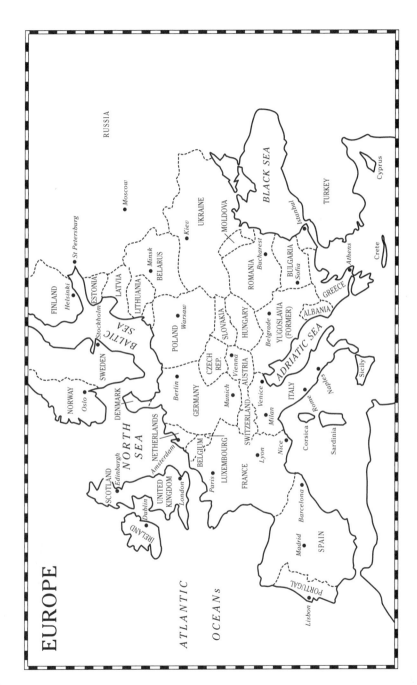

EUROPE

⸺ BIOGRAPHIES ⸺

W. H. Auden—English-born poet who achieved fame in the 1930s.

St. Augustine—First archbishop of Canterbury. He founded the Christian church in southern England around 597.

Francis Bacon—17th century statesman in England, he is remembered in literary terms for the insightful and worldly wisdom of his writings, as well as his superior command of the English language.

Gaston Bachelard—20th century French master of nonfiction prose and philosopher of science.

James Baldwin—American essayist, novelist, and playwright who is remembered for his passionate views on the subject of race in America in the late 1950s and early 1960s. *Go Tell It On the Mountain* (1953) is considered his finest work.

Catherine Drinker Brown—American historical biographer known for her partly fictionalized biographies.

Robert Browning—Major English poet of the Victorian age, remembered for his skill at writing dramatic monologue and psychological portraiture.

Lord Byron—English Romantic poet whose poetry and personal charisma were revered throughout Europe.

Lewis Carroll—English photographer and novelist who achieved acclaim as the author of *Alice's Adventures in Wonderland* (1865) and *Through the Looking-Glass* (1871).

Willa Cather—American novelist noted for her depictions of frontier life on the American plains in the 19th century.

Viscount de Chateaubriand—One of France's first Romantic writers, de Chateaubriand also served as a diplomat, and was considered a strong influence on the youth of his day. He was the preeminent literary figure in France in the early 19th century.

Samuel Taylor Coleridge—English Romantic lyrical poet and philosopher. Lyrical Ballads, which he wrote with William Wordsworth, is considered the work that ushered in the English Romantic movement.

Cyril Connolly—English critic and novelist, as well as the founder and editor of Horizon, a magazine focused on contemporary literature that had a great influence in Britain in its time (1939-1950).

Eugene Delacroix—French Romantic painter, considered a master in the use of color. He influenced the development of both Impressionist and Postimpressionist painters.

Gabriel Fielding—20th century American writer.

Gustave Flaubert—French novelist considered the master of the realist school of French literature. Best known for his masterpiece, *Madame Bovary* (1857).

E. M. Forster—Member of the Bloomsbury group of English writers, artists, and philosophers. Forster was a novelist, essayist, social and literary critic who is noted for his novels *Howards End* (1910) and *A Passage to India* (1924).

Andre Gide—French writer who received the Nobel Prize for literature in 1947.

William Hazlitt—English writer revered for his humanistic essays. His straightforward writing style, which lacks any pretension, is esteemed for the brilliant intellect it reveals.

Ernest Hemingway—American novelist and short-story writer who was awarded the Nobel Prize for literature in 1954. He is noted as one of the most influential writers of the 20th century; his works include *The Sun Also Rises* (1926) and *For Whom the Bell Tolls* (1940).

Samuel Johnson—English critic, biographer, essayist, poet, and lexicographer, he is considered one of the major figures of 18th century life and letters.

Alfred Kazin—American critic and writer noted for his studies of modern American literature as well as his autobiographical writings, which explored his life as a Russian Jewish immigrant in America.

Barbara Kingsolver—Contemporary American novelist whose works include *The Bean Trees* (1988).

Selma Lagerlof—The winter of the Nobel Prize in Literature in 1909, she was the first woman as well as the first Swedish writer to do so.

Susanne K. Langer—American philosopher who wrote on linguistics and aesthetics.

W. Somerset Maugham—English novelist and short-story writer whose style is characterized by clear prose, cosmopolitan settings, and a keen look at the workings of human nature. His works include *Of Human Bondage* (1915) and *The Razor's Edge* (1944).

Henry Miller—U.S. writer and expatriate who is known for his mid-20th-century autobiographical novels which often candidly addressed the subject of sex. His works were banned in the United States until the 1960s but were available in France, where he resided.

Anaïs Nin—French author of novels and short stories, she is remembered most for her eight published volumes of her personal diaries.

Marcel Proust—French novelist who wrote *Remembrance of Things Past* (1913-27), a seven-volume novel based on his life.

Jules Renard—Late 19th century French writer whose works are characterized by a grim humor and a simple, stripped-down prose.

Jean-Paul Sartre—French novelist, playwright, and philosopher, known for his magnum opus, *Being and Nothingness,* in which he expounded on existential themes. Awarded the Nobel Prize for Literature in 1964, he chose to decline it.

Gertrude Stein—Expatriate American writer who, along with her companion, Alice B. Toklas, hosted a Paris salon between World Wars I and II that attracted such leading artists and writers as Pablo Picasso, Ezra Pound, and Ernest Hemingway.

H. D. Thoreau—American essayist, poet, and Transcendentalist writer acclaimed for his masterwork, *Walden* (1854), as well as for his vigorous advocation of civil liberties in the mid-19th century.